MAKING THE
BASKETBALL
TEAM

Get Off The Bench and Into The Game

by Lane Czaplinski

Quality Sports Publications

MAKING THE
BASKETBALL
TEAM

Get Off
The Bench
and Into
The Game

by Lane Czaplinski

Photography by
Scott Irwig

Foreword by Roy Williams

Cover, "Jason" and
instructional photos by
Scott Irwig

Cover designed by
Mick McCay

For information write:

Quality Sports Publications
24 Buysse Drive
Coal Valley, IL 61240
(800) 464-1116
(309) 234-5016

Duane Brown, Project Director
Melinda Brown, Designer
Susan Smith, Editor
Scott Irwig, Photographer

Printed in the U.S.A.

ISBN 1-885758-08-1

Dedicated to those names who were never called, when choosing sides for basketball.

Contents

Foreword 11

Acknowledgements 13

Chapter One: Trying Out 14

   Hang Time 14

   A Note From the Author 15

   The First Day 16

   Understanding Tryouts 18

   What's Your Situation? 21

   Rank Yourself 22

   The School: What Happened Last Year? 23

   Does the Coach Know Who You Are? 24

   Exploit Your Talents 24

   Hustle Spot 25

   Meet Jason 26

Chapter Two: Skills 28

   Making Practice Your Game 28

A Typical Basketball Tryout/Practice   29

    Free Shooting   30

    Two Line Lay-Ups   34

    Fastbreak... 3 on 2/2 on 1   39

    Defensive Sliding   45

    One-On-One Defense... Pressure   49

    Stations   57

    Free Throws and Water   73

    Scrimmaging... Get The Ball   76

    Conditioning   103

    Remarks   118

Chapter 3 Getting Ready   124

    Individual Practice   125

    Competition   125

    Off-Season Conditioning   126

    Practice Chart   128

    What Happens to Jason?   132

About The Author   138

Index   140

Foreword

Dear Readers:

As an individual who has spent his life in basketball, I have had the privilege of watching scores of young men and women fulfill their dreams of becoming basketball players for their junior high, high school or college. I also see the tremendous disappointment of those who never make the team. Former Kansas basketball player Lane Czaplinski made the team because he worked hard and believed in his ability to play the game. Lane has written an excellent book for young men and women trying to make the basketball team and fulfill their dreams. He offers a unique perspective, giving specific advice on how to approach training for tryouts, concentrating on both physical and mental fundamentals crucial to achieving success on the basketball court. I also found this to be a good book for those already on a team wanting to improve their skills.

I know his book will be helpful to all who read it. And why not? Lane is a perfect example of someone who used his own advice and made the team. He is a fine individual who has done a tremendous service to young men and women who love the game. Be sure to read every page.

Roy Williams
University of Kansas Basketball Head Coach

Acknowledgements

It is fitting that I start off by recognizing the people who made this project possible. I'm fortunate to have them on my team.

Every writer dreams of having a publisher as responsive as Quality Sports and working with good, talented people like Duane and Melinda Brown.

Margot Maley not only has the perfect sounding name for an agent, but she backs it up by plugging away on the writer's behalf.

Scott Irwig's photographs were an unexpected bonus and I appreciate his patience and hard work.

Whether it was the opportunity to hold a championship trophy or the support to get a book published, Roy Williams has always given me a tremendous deal. Thank you.

I'm in debt to both Danny Manning and Dr. David Cook for giving me a lift on their coattails.

I still owe Jeannie Mellinger many dinners for her careful reading, thoughtful insights and clever writing. Thanks for having Sam read it, too.

Many others did a fine job of editing this book and offering many suggestions: Fred Woodward, Ginger Ireton, Jennifer Jacquinot, Mike Nelson, Bob Miller, Joe Coles, Rick Keltner, Stacey Reed and Bob Murphy.

I couldn't have gotten better models for this project than Byron Myrick, Michael Norwood and "Jason."

Mike Maddox's legal expertise made foreign territory feel safer.

Tony Harvey came through in the clutch and was extremely accommodating. Thanks to Carl for staying late.

My former teammates and coaches exist in these pages and I thank them for teaching me many lessons.

From Honolulu to Boston to Lawrence, Kansas, I am supported by a solid foundation of family and friends. Despite the distance that separates us, they have all managed to stay with me. In particular, Manisha Sharma, Mike Norwood, Steve Holmstrom and David Shepard all keep me upright and walking straight. Their support is immeasurable and so is my regard for them.

Judy Moore has always been the consummate patron saint and taming Pops is a neat trick, too.

The knowledge and spirit found in this book were always present while growing up because I had my father, George Czaplinski. His steady words of encouragement still whisper in my ear and his influence has shaped my life like no other.

I will not be happier than when I first show this book to my mother, Jane Czaplinski. Her unwavering support is only topped by her example of living with love and kindness.

Finally, I should have put the name of Jackie Davis on the front cover before my own. Her talent of "making things happen" impacted virtually every phase of this project, and thus, I am forever grateful.

Lane Czaplinski

CHAPTER ONE

TRYING OUT

"Much has been made of the story that, as a sophomore in high school, Jordan was cut from his school's basketball team. It's part of the legend. But think about it for a minute. It wasn't a legend for him then. He was a boy who was told that he wasn't good enough...

'I went to my room and I closed the door and I cried," Jordan said. "For a while I couldn't stop. Even though there was no one else home at the time, I kept the door shut. It was important to me that no one hear me or see me. For about two weeks, every boy who had tried out for the basketball team knew what day the cut list was going to go up," he said. "We knew that it was going to be posted in the gym in the morning. So that morning we all went in there, and the list was up. I had a friend – his name was Leroy Smith – and we went in to look at the list together. We stood there and looked for our names. If your name was on the list, you were still on the team. If your name wasn't on the list, you were cut. Leroy's name was on the list. He made it. Mine wasn't on the list. I looked and looked for my name. It was almost as if I thought that if I didn't stop looking, it would be there.

I went through the day numb. I sat through my classes. I had to wait until after school to go home. That's when I hurried to my house and I closed the door of my room and I cried so hard. It was all I wanted – to play on that team.'"

– From *Hang Time*
by Michael Jordan &
Bob Greene

A Note From The Author

My name is not Michael, not Larry and definitely not Magic. I've never been bigger than 5'10," 175 lbs. My arms and legs are too short for my body and I have small hands. No one has or ever will mistake me for an NBA All-Star, yet I feel extremely lucky for the success I enjoyed during my basketball career. When I look back over my career, which spanned from grade school to college, I think I am fortunate that things turned out the way they did. Considering how much people talk about basketball players needing to be tall or fast or able to jump high, it's strange how little these things really matter now in comparison to the lessons I learned while playing the game.

Too many people are concerned with factors no one can control: how tall someone is or how many times someone's name appears in the newspaper. Young players need to spend more time concentrating on all the skills that are within their power to improve. This book discusses all the different ways players can focus their heads and their hearts on achieving their dreams.

The First Day

The 3 p.m. bell rings. Everyone exits class for the day and strolls nonchalantly towards the locker room. *Gotta look cool, not too excited. Don't want anyone to think I'm nervous.* The gym becomes chaotic with screams as the dressed players make their way onto the floor. Pandemonium reigns. Balls bounce all over the place. Kids run them down and hoist them toward the goal. When there isn't a ball to chase, some just chase each other. Those who played last year act too good for all of this. Some of them sit sprawled in the bleachers while others sit on the ground as if they're stretching (everyone knows that to actually stretch would be out of place). Most of the kids, however, look kind of lost and unsure. Some shoot an occasional shot when a ball rolls to them but otherwise they stand off to the side or under the basket, hoping a ball will rebound to them. With arms outstretched overhead, they stand there hoping that all goes well and that they make the team and get to play a lot and score some points. But there are just too many hands reaching, grabbing for the ball and none of the rebounds go their way. *How am I ever going to get warmed up if I can't even get a ball to shoot?* Doesn't matter anyway. The coach blows his whistle and yells for everyone to sit in the stands. Everyone shuffles towards the sideline as the first day is about to begin.

Every year the majority of kids who try to play basketball come away from the experience feeling bitter and disillusioned, and these feelings start from the first day of tryouts. Tryouts are more than the first day of the basketball season. It is the beginning of a larger process that is both confusing and frustrating. The confusion builds with time and continues through practices into the actual games. These feelings are not limited to players who get cut or don't get to play much. Even kids who experience some success usually finish the season saying they wish they had done better but that they never understood what was expected of them. This common thought is expressed by more players than one might think. Probably the biggest complaint of unhappy basketball players is not having a chance to prove oneself. Not getting in the game or not getting passed the ball or just not getting much of a chance to show one's talent can all lead to disappointment. Given all this frustration, it's not difficult to see how much players with varying ability and talent actually have in common. They all want a fair shot at achieving their goals while at the same time managing to keep the coach happy and off their backs.

Understanding Tryouts

Of all the times where a person has a chance to prove what they can do, tryouts are probably the hardest time for accomplishing this crucial goal.

1. More players try out than attend a typical practice, so there is less time for individuals to demonstrate their skills.
2. Since each player wants to do well, it's usually a highly competitive free-for-all atmosphere featuring very little teamwork and cooperation. Don't be too surprised if no one passes you the ball while you're standing all alone under the basket.
3. The coach has only one set of eyes and lots of bodies to consider in a very short amount of time. You may do everything perfect and the coach might not ever notice. Can you really blame him or her? It's hard for one set of eyes to see the actions of 50 players. For this very reason, the coach will probably have a good idea of who will be on the roster before tryouts ever start.

What all of this means is that most of the time, very little is actually accomplished during tryouts. Coaches feel like they can't do much until they have selected their actual team. Players are mad because they hardly get to touch the ball or perform in a situation where their talents stand out. These feelings lead to a lot of unhappy people standing around not trying very hard, and as a result, nothing much really happens. **When nothing really happens during practice, the advantage goes to the superstars, veterans and athletes.** Every time a player on the brink (by this, I mean a player who might not make the team or might not get much playing time) does not stand out in some manner, the advantage goes to the superstars, the veterans and the athletes. The reason is simple. Everything being equal, coaches will pick and choose the most talented players on the court first. Then they'll choose the players with the most experience, or perhaps before ever doing this, they'll choose the best athletes. The tallest players. That kid who can jump out of the gym. That little waterbug no one can catch. So if everyone is playing poorly, the coach is more likely to judge the talent pool by talent, experience and athletic ability even if everyone is playing equally bad. If you don't fit into one of these categories, and most players who want to play basketball do not, then you're immediately placed behind all of the players who do.

Consider these situations:

Situation #1: Everyone has been doing the same drill for the last 10 minutes. The coach has been talking a lot, stopping and starting the activity to give instructions. As a result, no one really stands out because the coach is always interrupting.

Advantage: superstars, veterans and athletes

Situation #2: Nothing is happening. The coach leaves the court to call home and say he or she will be late for dinner. The assistant coaches are standing in a corner talking about going out for a few beers that night. The players are supposed to be doing a drill but because no one in charge appears to be watching, everyone stops doing the drill and starts joking around.

Advantage: superstars, veterans and athletes

Given that tryouts are a tough situation in which to come out ahead, you have to figure out a strategy that will help you achieve exactly what you want. **You must have a master plan.** Too many young basketball players show up on the first day of practice with high hopes but no idea how they'll make their dreams come true. You can't simply play and practice a couple of weeks before the season and then just sort of show up on the first day saying: "Here I am everybody. Can I play too?"

It is almost impossible to play and look like a good basketball player when you haven't been practicing and have no idea what to expect. All too often the only time a player is noticed is when something negative happens: a player makes a bad pass that goes out the gym door, out the building, and rolls down a hill into a mud puddle. This is not how anyone wants to be noticed, but you will never be noticed by anyone if you don't figure out how to be in the **right place**, at the **right time**, doing the **right thing**. Don't confuse this with kissing up to the coach. It's a matter of taking advantage of every opportunity you can by making all the seemingly unimportant little things count for something more. You must learn to **make the little things big**. Everyone tries to score their way on to the team and into the starting line-up, but there are few real opportunities to actually do this. The best basketball players do a variety of little things that no one else ever notices: setting screens, outrunning everyone down the floor, yelling encouragement to teammates, making a steal, helping a teammate on defense. This book helps you figure out how to take advantage of each moment. Use it to figure out a strategy of all the things you can do to make yourself have a better chance of accomplishing your goal. There are so many mental parts to playing good basketball that there's never an excuse for the words "I'm too short or too slow." No matter what anyone says, you control your improvement as a basketball player and whether or not you achieve your basketball dreams. Nothing will aid you more in this quest than using your head and your heart.

What's Your Situation?

A major step to accomplishing your dreams is figuring out exactly what they are. Fantasizing about accepting the NCAA Championship Trophy on behalf of your team is fine; it's actually wonderful, but you must also take a realistic look at your situation as it stands now. How are you going to get to that championship trophy from here?

You **will not** become a great basketball player overnight but you **can** *improve*. Expecting too much too fast will only lead to frustration and giving up before you give yourself a real chance. Improving each day is the key.

> Improve One Level At A Time...
> * Never Played Before
> * Gets Cut
> * Barely Makes Team
> * Never Gets To Play
> * Plays
> * Starter
> * All–Star

Rank Yourself

How many players are competing for how many spots? Of all the people you know trying out for the team, rank the top fifteen players. Where do you rank? If you don't rank in the top fifteen, how far away are you from this group and what do you think it will take to get there? Which players are your main competition? What are the strengths and weaknesses of each player?

1. _____   9. _____

2. _____   10. _____

3. _____   11. _____

4. _____   12. _____

5. _____   13. _____

6. _____   14. _____

7. _____   15. _____

8. _____

Think about your angle. What is going to make you stand apart from the crowd? Your desire? Your practice habits? Your enthusiasm? Your defense? Your passing?

The School

A father recently told me of his son who was cut from the high school basketball team as a senior. According to him, that was the only high school team in the state on which his son wasn't good enough to play. Indeed, that team did go on to win the state championship, meaning that there were talented players on the team, making for tough competition as far as spots and playing time goes. Also, it was a particularly large school meaning there was a lot of competition for just a few spots.

Some schools are the exact opposite of this. Everyone who wants to play gets a chance. There's still a pecking order, however. Some players play every minute of every game while others are lucky to get a few seconds of action.

No matter which of these situations applies to you, it is self-defeating to look around at other schools and figure that there's a better situation somewhere else, that shots would be made a lot easier if one were to go there instead. In most cases this is simply untrue. Kids all over have to fight their way on to the team and into games. Besides, in most cases kids don't merely have the luxury of choosing the school that best suits their basketball skills. You must make your present school and situation work to fulfill your dreams.

What happened last year?

It's hard going into tryouts having no idea what to expect. Therefore, you should talk to players who played on the team last year. What were tryouts and practices like? What is the coach like? What does he or she expect?

What drills did they do? Remember that each player has a unique version of the team and the coach and what try-outs were like. Things may be different this year. Talking about it will at least get you thinking about what may happen and what you need to do to prepare.

Does The Coach Know Who You Are?

Sounds like a stupid question, huh? Then why do so many kids show up for the first day of practice without having ever introduced themselves to the coach before-hand? Again, I'm not talking about giving Christmas presents so the coach will reward you with a starting position and the green light on three-pointers. It just makes sense that the coach knows who you are before practices ever start. The coach knows all of the best play-ers on a first-name basis. There's nothing wrong with introducing yourself to the coach before tryouts ever start. Introducing yourself the day before the first day of practice is not good enough. Ideally, the coach should see you playing with the other main players from last year and/or working out in the weight room during the sum-mer. If the two of you never happen to be in a conversa-tion, you should just go up and say hello. Let the coach know that you're excited about the upcoming season and you're playing every day, working on your game. After all, this should be the truth.

Exploit your talent

Use any advantage God gave you: height, quickness, jumping ability, speed, strength. Some players have tremendous physical talent, yet never fully realize what their bodies can do.

If you're taller than most people, get every rebound you can. If you're stronger than everyone else, push the tall person out of the way and get rebounds. If you're quicker than most, drive around the strong and tall people. If you jump well, then jump over these jokers. Of course, if you've got a head, then just outthink them all.

Hustle Spot

It's hard to figure out exactly why or how, but every year on almost every team, some kid hustles his or her way to a spot on the team. These players aren't hard to identify because their scarred knees from rolling around all over the floor usually give them away. Some of them even become famous for strange kamikaze dives into the bleachers, plays that look spectacular but are probably unnecessary. Sometimes these hustlers are kind of annoying because they're always jumping on top of you, reaching for the ball like some sort of excited dog or something. But when all is said or done, at least one of these players earns a spot on the team or starting line-up because the coach just can't afford to let that kind of effort and determination go.

Patrick Ewing was such a bad player at age 13 that he was always the last player chosen for pick-up games even though he was 6'8".

Meet Jason

At 15, Jason is a late-comer to basketball considering that most of his friends started playing three and four years earlier. He was never that interested in sports until two summers ago when he started shooting around on his neighbor's goal. Eventually he started playing games with kids in the neighborhood and even though they were older, he played well and continued to improve daily. One of his best friends convinced him to try out for the team last year but he didn't make it. Now a year later, Jason is trying again. He's kind of quiet and thinks no one will want him around, especially since the kids who'll probably be on this year's team were part of the team last year that won the league championship. He decides to go for it even though he isn't sure what to expect. We'll check in with Jason throughout the book to see how he's getting along.

SKILLS

CHAPTER TWO

Making Practice Your Game

Only five players get to play at one time, leaving more or less 10 players on the sideline watching and usually many times that number watching from the stands not having made the team. These frustrated players all say similar things: "If all we ever do is practice, how am I supposed to prove myself?" or "How can they cut me when I never got a chance to show what I can do in real games?"

When players don't play much or don't even make the team, games themselves don't really matter much. Practices and tryouts replace games in importance because that's when these players actually play and have the opportunity to prove themselves.

Players who expect to score their way onto the team playing in games end up disappointed because instead of playing and scoring, they spend half of the time in defensive drills sliding from baseline to baseline. This is why understanding what goes on in practices is extremely important, so you have some idea of what to expect and can figure out a strategy for improving your chances.

A Typical Basketball Tryout/Practice
Day 1
> Free shooting
> Two line lay-ups
> 3 on 2/2 on 1
> Defensive sliding (group)
> One-on-one
> Stations:
>> 3 on 3 (team defense)
>> Rebounding
>> Ball-handling
>> Shooting
> Free throws and water
> Scrimmage
> Conditioning
> Remarks

Does any of this look familiar? What is a two-on-one? What do I do on stations? This is how a typical tryout or practice looks. **This section of the book is arranged like the above practice plan.** The basic skills you need to play basketball are all here. They are presented in the way you are likely to use them in a tryout or practice. Learning the skills in this manner will give you a better idea of what to expect, and by knowing what to expect, you'll be able to take advantage of the situation and make it work out in your favor.

Free Shooting

Every time you step on the court, you must be ready to play hard and do anything possible to become a better player. Warming up before practice is no exception. While everyone else is firing 35-footers, show you're serious about playing. Hustle onto the court. Try to be the first player in the gym. The best players always **go early and stay late.** Be the first to show up and the last to leave. Work on the shots you've been practicing. Always start close to the basket whether you're learning a new skill or you're just warming up. Develop your rhythm by not being concerned with distance. Shoot as many shots as you can. Some coaches have things for players to do when they first warm up: stretching exercises or jumping rope, for example. Be aware if there are any instructions.

Building Your Shot

Stand directly in front of the goal, only three or four feet away. Balance the ball in your strong hand with your arm and elbow pointed in the direction of the goal the same way a dart player points their elbow in the direction of a dart board. With the ball balanced and your knees bent, extend your arm up towards the goal as if you're actually going to put your hand in the goal. Jerking or snapping the follow-through downward causes a lack of touch.

Try going for height. Creeping the ball over the front of the rim is much too tentative. Pros use lots of arch on their shots and so should you. Just for practice sake, see how high you can shoot it using good form. The more you bend your knees, the easier it is to achieve good arch. Keep using only your shooting hand while learning because it ensures that the ball is balanced. Stay close to the hoop working at shooting with lots of height (arch). See how many shots you can make in a row. Try to make 10 straight. Then 20 straight. It's not as easy as it looks but if you can't hit 10 in a row from close range, how can you expect those results from further out?

Now try placing your off hand on the side of the ball. It steadies the ball but it doesn't hold it up. Balance the ball in your shooting hand and place the off hand on the side. NOW STOP. Without changing anything or moving, take the non-shooting hand off the ball. If the ball drops, you didn't have it balanced and were relying on the off hand too much.

Staying close, shoot a shot with only one hand, and then, shoot a shot using both hands. Another with one hand. Another with two hands. Alternate back and forth until each type of shot feels the same.

Increase your range or the distance from which you can shoot comfortably by slowly moving back a step at a time. Shoot a short shot from in front of the goal. Take a step back and shoot the same high, soft shot. Take a step in and shoot. Take a step back and shoot. Do this until both shots feel the same regardless from where you shoot them. As it feels more and more comfortable, take another step back. Each time you miss or the shot feels uncomfortable, take a step towards the basket.

Jason...Too Cool

Three of the team's best players can't participate during the first week of the season because they were caught ditching school. Is there an opportunity? Of course there is, yet Jason just glides through stretching, acting nonchalant like everyone else. He doesn't realize that each time he blends in with the crowd and fails to make an identity for himself, it becomes all the more likely that he'll be forgotten when the coaches sit down to figure out the roster.

Two Line Lay-Ups

This drill is a good example of how to **make the little things big.** Nearly every team in the country does this drill or another type of lay-up drill that is just as basic. The directions are usually pretty simple: One line shoots lay-ups and then goes to the other line, the other line rebounds the basketball and passes it to the lay-up line and then goes to the back of that line. Yet all the time, players see this drill and say, "Ah man, that's easy. I can do that," and proceed to just flop through the drill, not really paying attention to the little parts. Don't miss opportunities to show all the different skills you have, no matter how small they may seem.

- Try getting to the front of the line – it shows you're excited to play. If you don't want to shoot first, then get in the front of the rebounding line.
- Jump up and get the rebound like it's a game. Never, ever let the ball hit the ground.
- Pivot towards the receiver in the shooting line. If they're running in for a lay-up, hit them with a bounce pass. If two balls are being used and the receiver is still in line, throw a strong, crisp pass. Coaches can spot correctly thrown passes anywhere. Of course, they can spot poor passes even easier. Those are the ones that are thrown out the door of the gym or hit the coach in the back of the head. You probably won't have a very good season if you hit the coach with too many of your passes.
- Run, don't walk to the back of the other line. It's easier to run up the middle as opposed to the outside of the drill, but listen to which way your coach

prefers and do that. You don't want to look out of place and like you aren't paying attention to what's going on.

- Approach the basket at an angle that makes it easy to use the backboard on the shot. Catch the ball on the run close enough to the basket where you don't have to dribble and can shoot the lay-up directly off the pass. This is a more advanced method and it looks better.

- **Put the sucker in the hole. Many coaches use lay-ups as an instant cutting device. They figure if a player can't make the closest, easiest shot there is, then there isn't much of a chance they'll make any thing. Plus, lay-ups usually indicate how much experience a player has, the more awkward lay-ups pointing out those players not comfortable with the ball.**

- This drill might be extended to full court, meaning that you might have to make more passes or take more dribbles than described here. That's fine. Just take your time and concentrate on what needs to be done. You can still go hard and fast but don't rush yourself. Practicing your skills a lot helps you perform quickly and efficiently without feeling uncomfortable.

Lay-Ups

Learn lay-ups from the basket out, not starting away from the basket. Start with your strong hand on that side of the basket about a foot or two away from the goal. With the ball in your strong hand, raise the ball as if you're going to shoot and at the same time bring the same knee to your chest. If the ball is in your right hand, imagine a short string from your right elbow to your right knee. Each time your right arm goes up, so does your right knee.

Continue to shoot from the same spot – strong hand/same knee up – trying to put the ball nice and high on the backboard. Pros use all of the backboard instead of just creeping the ball barely over the top of the rim. Isaiah Thomas, who probably had one of the nicest lay-ups in NBA history, really laid his ball high on the glass so it fell through cleanly.

While learning to shoot this way, shoot your lay-ups overhanded. Later, as you become more comfortable and shoot your lay-ups with greater speed, you'll probably learn to shoot them underhanded unless your coach says otherwise.

Now try the footwork. Take one step back. Assuming  again that you are shooting right-handed lay-ups (the opposite for lefties), step out with your left foot and then shoot with your right hand/right knee up. Try it again going slowly. Say to yourself, "left, shoot." After a few times, take two steps back. This time your footwork will be, "right, left, shoot." Don't worry if this is traveling or not...this is practice and you're learning. Back up another two steps. This time add the drib- ble which will make your foot-

Footwork for shooting a right-handed lay-up
"Right... Left...Shoot..."

work "dribble, right, left, shoot." Go very slowly. The key here is feeling comfortable picking up your dribble and taking the two steps ("right, left") before shooting. You get two steps (some people call it one and a half steps) after you pick up your dribble before it becomes traveling.

It doesn't matter after a while how many dribbles you take because the end will always be the same, "right, left, shoot."

IMPORTANT – Switch to the opposite side and develop the other handed lay-up. Don't call it your weak hand because you want to eventually shoot all your lay-ups the same way no matter which hand you use. Dr. J and Michael Jordan were great because they could switch to the other hand to get their lay-ups off. Simply reverse the footwork ("dribble, left, right, shoot").

Knowing how to shoot lay-ups off the pass as opposed to the dribble is important because in many situations and practice drills, you'll receive a pass in stride and there will be no reason to dribble because you're already close. Picture Anfernee Hardaway dribbling down the middle of the court on a fast break. Shaquille O'Neil is on one side and you are on the other side. Hardaway won't pass the ball until the last instant so the defense won't have time to react. You'll be going fast enough and be close enough that you'll only need to lay the ball in the basket instead of wasting time dribbling. Your footwork will be (assuming you're on the right side), "catch-right, left, shoot." Rehearse this by having someone pass you the ball as you break towards the basket. Remember to stay nice and wide of the goal to give yourself a comfortable angle for laying the ball off the backboard.

Pretty Is As Pretty Does

Many coaches talk about approaching the basket at a certain angle or jumping high instead of long jumping. The reality is that you need to become good at shooting many different types of lay-ups at different angles with either hand. A good rule, though, is always shoot the most basic lay-up possible in practice drills. Players who try to be pretty instead of effective are only making life difficult for themselves. An even more basic rule is to make all of your lay-ups!

Quickness Drill

Standing on the free-throw line, dribble in for a lay-up, rebound the ball, run back to the free-throw line, and repeat. See how many lay-ups you can make in 30 seconds. Don't be fooled by how simple it sounds. Talented players can do this somewhere between 6-8 times.

Fast Break... 3 On 2 / 2 On 1

Understanding fast breaks is important because almost all teams practice them even if they don't run the ball much in games. Often times, the hardest part about fast break drills is understanding the coach's complicated instructions. Many times they make drills appear much harder than they actually are. These can be listening tests as much as they are basketball drills. Listen closely to the instructions. Another good idea before tryouts ever start is to talk to players who played the year before to find out exactly what goes on in tryouts. Ask them what types of drills were done the previous year and what the coach looks for. You'll still need to listen to the coach's instructions (the veteran player might have given bad descriptions) but at least you'll have a feel for some of the things that might happen.

As an example, let's use a common fast break drill called **3 on 2/2 on 1**. Going down the court there will be three offensive players against two defenders. Coming back up the court, there will be two offensive players against one defender.

- To start the drill, someone will usually shoot the ball so the players have to rebound it before they actually start the break. Sometimes there will even be someone for the defense to block out for the rebound. Be sure to get the rebound before it touches the ground or the wrong people get it.
- If you get the rebound, turn without dribbling and pass it to the first open teammate running up the floor (throw an outlet pass which is described later in the book). The coach will probably make clear where the first pass needs to go.
- Get the ball to the middle of the floor. This prevents the defense from predicting which way the offense will go.
- Get ahead of the ball. If you don't have the ball, run hard to get ahead of it. There are three fast break lanes: right, middle and left. Get to one of these.
- Know what you're going to do before you catch the ball. This rule applies to all situations but it is especially true of fast breaks. Know ahead of time what the play will be.
- Always step in the direction you pass the ball because you might get it right back.

Fast Break Situations/2 on 1

Take it to the basket – hard!

Two offensive players versus one defensive player.

Whenever there is only one defensive person guarding the basket against two or more players, the offense should get a lay-up. Staying close to your teammate (about a lane's width apart) makes guarding the two of you much more difficult. If you have the ball, dribble all the way in for a lay-up unless the defense stops you, at which point, you pass to your teammate. Make sure the defense really stops you and isn't just faking or they'll probably steal your pass.

Fast Break Situations/3 on 2

Make the easy play – take the short jumper.

Whenever there are two or more people back on defense, think about going for a short jump shot. With two people on defense, one person will almost always be guarding the basket which makes lay-ups difficult. Go for the easy play. It's much better to take a short comfortable shot on the lane instead of turning the ball over on some wild drive to the basket. Pull up for a short jump shot if you receive the ball on the right or left wing. If it's not open, simply dump it back to the passer. If you are the ball-handler in the middle, drive hard to the free-throw line. Most of the time someone will pick you up, leaving one of your other two teammates open (if no one picks you up at the free-throw line, stand up and hit the jumper). Remember to step in the direction you pass in case your teammate is covered and wants to pass the ball back. Be prepared to shoot in this case because you'll be wide open. Follow the shot and rebound – three players should always score against just two.

Jason...Fast Break Success

Jason does well in the fast break drill. In one sequence, he gets a rebound, scores and then steals the ball on defense. The coach tells him 'nice job' and that he needs to do that all the time. Jason isn't sure what to make of this comment but doesn't have much time to think about it as the next drill begins.

Take Advantage Of All the Opportunities

Even though you may be doing a fast break drill, you have a tremendous opportunity to stand out playing defense. Think about it. There will usually be one less defender so any time the defense stops the offense from scoring, everyone will consider it great defense. Plus, you'll usually have a chance to take it back down on offense if you steal the ball.

- Force the offense into making one extra pass or taking one more dribble than they want. The longer they handle the ball, the more likely it is they'll make mistakes.

- The first person (or only person) back on defense should protect the basket – don't give up an easy lay-up. Fake at the ball-handler and make them try something difficult. This is an excellent opportunity for taking an offensive charge.

- The second person back on defense (two people now) guards the ball and tries to break the ball-handler's momentum. Make them pass the ball. On the pass, run back and guard the basket because your teammate under the basket will guard the player catching the pass. Talk and let your teammate know exactly what you're going to do. "I've got the ball, I've got the ball. You take the first pass."

Defensive Sliding

Sliding is the quickest way to move while playing defense because it allows you to move in any direction at any given moment. Becoming comfortable with sliding will not only improve your defense significantly but it will make you more comfortable performing defensive drills in practice. Most coaches have a love affair with defensive sliding, and as a result, make their teams spend hour after hour crouched over sliding from baseline to baseline. Many defensive drills are performed by the entire group at one time. Group drills are great because you get to show how hard you work and how well you follow directions as compared to everyone else. Concentrate on the instructions given by the coach or you will be the only one in the gym sliding to your left while everyone else is going right. Don't hide in the back of the group, either. Get up in the front where the coach can see how hard you get after it.

Stance

Start in a good stance. Many coaches put players in strange robot-like positions and say, "now play defense," and the player can barely move because all they can think about is how dorky they look. Bend your knees and get low. By hitting your palms on the floor and staying in that low position, you can react more quickly than if you're standing up straight. The tricky part is keeping your head up while you're in such a low position so you can see the entire court.

*Hitting the floor... puts you in a good
defensive stance.*

Step-Slides

This drill is very slow and deliberate. Start with one leg
back, one to two feet in back of the other one. Hit the
ground and get in a defensive position. Step slowly with
your back foot, the heel touching first and pulling the
toes down. Each step goes heel to toe. Say it to yourself,
"heel-toe, heel-toe." The back or "heel-toe" leg drags the
front foot. STAY LOW. Once you come to a side line,
change directions by throwing your front elbow back in
the direction you want to go. This will turn your foot
and entire body for you. To change directions while sliding, remember, throw the front elbow back in the direc-

Heel: The back foot takes a step with the heel touching the floor first.

Toe: The heel of the back foot pulls the toes to the floor.

Slide: The toes of the back foot, in turn, pull the front foot in a sliding motion. Do this drill in slow motion, emphasizing staying low to the floor.

tion you want to go. Head down the court from side line to side line in a zig-zag pattern. Go to half court and come back. Do the drill as if you're in slow motion, concentrating on staying low. This really strengthens the muscles in your legs for playing defense.

Quick Slides

Slide back and forth across the lane as fast as you can. It should take no more than two slides to cover the entire lane (maybe three if you're smaller). Do not touch or cross your feet while sliding. See how many times you can cross the lane in 30 seconds.

One-On-One Defense

One-on-one scares many players because getting beat badly by the offense means you got burned for everyone else to see. The idea is easy to understand – one player tries to stop the other from scoring or driving by them. The key to playing good one-on-one defense is applying lots of pressure against the offense from the very beginning. This makes the offense uncomfortable and forces them to do something they'd rather not. Pressure is the defense's way of controlling the offense and determining what the ball-handler does. Otherwise, the offense can stand there comfortably and make the play they want.

1. Pressure – bother the ball.
2. Retreat – react to the drive by beating them to where they're going.

Try to get an arm's length away from the person with the ball.

Arm's Length Away

A good general rule is get an arm's length away from the person with the ball . From this low stance, stick your closest arm straight out at the ball-handler like a fencer jabbing a sword – just be able to touch the player after straightening your arm out. If the ball-handler is quicker than you, compensate by getting a little further away. Staying lower than the person you're guarding gives you an advantage because it makes it harder for the offense to drive past you.

Get A Piece Of The Ball

It's surprising how many times you can actually touch the ball while the offense is holding it. Try hitting it as hard as you can without fouling. Think how nervous this makes the ball-handler. Picture how aggressive this makes you look.

Defensive Foot Position

The position of your feet helps keep the offense under control by forcing them in one direction. Remember the rule "belly-baseline" and your feet will always be in the right position. That is, whichever side of the floor the ball-handler is on, drop a leg back towards the basket pointing your belly button in the direction of that baseline. For example, if the ball is on the left side, you should have your left leg dropped back toward the basket. The only exception is if the ball-handler is in the middle of the court. Then keep your feet even so they can't drive straight at the goal. Once they move to one side or another, you can resume your "belly-baseline" stance.

Funneling the offense towards the baseline allows you

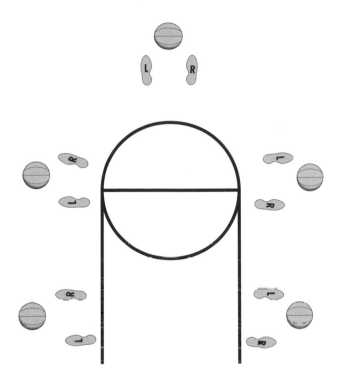

Defensive Foot Position

to use the baseline as a wall since the offense can't go out of bounds. **Never let a player drive by you on the baseline side.** This makes coaches go crazy because there's no help on that side if you let a player drive by. Cutting opponents off at the baseline forces them back towards the middle where there is help from other teammates.

Retreat

Pressure bothers the defense. You know they'll try to drive so anticipate that you'll have to beat them to where they want to go by sliding your feet quickly. Stay low as you're sliding. Standing up allows players to lean past you and go around.

Jason...Look Like A Basketball Player

Jason has a bad habit of standing too straight-legged. He needs to look like a basketball player. He needs to bend his knees and put more of an effort into anticipating the next play, the next opportunity. Each time he is caught unprepared and unable to react, it leaves the impression that he lacks experience and knowledge of the game.

Bump and Run

One of the hardest defensive situations for many players is guarding a player with the basketball for the length of the court. Many coaches do a poor job teaching full-court one-on-one defense. They put two players at the opposite end of the gym, give one player the ball, and tell the other to guard the ball to the other end of the floor. All they say is "slide," and if the defense starts to get beaten: "c'mon, slide those feet faster."

Successfully guarding a player the length of the court involves the same "bump and run" technique of a defensive player in football defending a wide receiver. The defensive back hits the receiver hard at the line of scrimmage, knocking the receiver off the intended route. This physical contact gives the defense a chance to turn and run to beat the offense to the pass from the quarterback.

It's the same play in basketball except the offense already has possession of the ball, that is, if you let them catch it. Before your opponent ever catches the ball, make sure you're good and close so when he or she does catch the ball, you'll be able to **bump** him or her by making an aggressive play on the ball which makes it harder for the ball-handler to face where they are going (Figure 1). And exactly what is an aggressive play? It's not a foul, but it's not a little flick at the wrist, either. Try to hit the ball hard. The ball-handler will react to the BUMP by driving up the floor as hard as possible. Knowing this beforehand, immediately turn and sprint to a spot in the path of the dribble so you can cut the player off (Figures 2 & 3). Remember, the defense is sprinting without a ball and the offense has to worry about dribbling as well. Since both of you are starting from the same spot on the floor, the defense should always be able to outrun the dribbler to a particular spot (Figure 4).

Full Court Defense Means You Run – Don't Just Slide.

Figure 1

Figure 2

Figure 3

Figure 4

Don't Let 'Em Catch It

Before the person you're guarding has the ball, you should make every effort not to let them stand there and catch the ball. If the offense doesn't catch it, you don't have to worry about guarding the ball. It is more of a matter of remembering to do it than anything else. You'll be surprised how little effort it takes to discourage the inbounder from throwing it to the person you're guarding. Simply put a hand up between the person trying to throw the ball inbounds and the person you're guarding. This is a tremendously effective defensive technique and it's rather simple. Just remember to do it.

They Don't Call Fouls In Tryouts And Practice

They just don't, at least not most of the time. So what, you committed a foul...big deal...everyone commits them. No one cares. Oh sure, the player you fouled might be irritated or the coach might yell to stop hacking but at least you aren't playing tentatively, letting other players do whatever they want while you stand helplessly by. Besides, coaches don't talk about it much but they like a player who won't back away from anyone.

> ## Match Up With Your Competition
>
> If there are players whom you consider to be your main competition in tryouts, then match up against them in drills. Don't go out of your way to do this or do it real obviously because it's not that important. But if there's a chance for you to beat a player everyone thinks is just as good as you, then go against them and prove you can more than hold your own.

Stations

Coaches like using stations because it allows them to drill their team on several skills at one time. Think of stations as a carnival with a different game at each booth. There is usually a coach at each station teaching a different fundamental to a group of players. After about five minutes, there will be a whistle and you'll switch to the next one. Think ahead of time about what the next station will be and be the first one out of your group to get to that station. Listen carefully to the coach's instructions. Again, these are great opportunities for showing how hard you work.

Station #1: Ball-Handling

The stories about Pistol Pete Maravich are legendary. He used to dribble everywhere he went. He dribbled in the aisle of the theater while watching movies. He dribbled while watching T.V. No wonder so many people consider him the greatest ball-handler the world has ever known.

Five Common Ball-Handling Drills

Practicing these five drills will make you a better ball-handler; plus drills like these are often used in tryouts to see who can handle the ball. Get a watch with a second hand and see how many of each you can do in 30 seconds. Keep your head up and don't look at the ball. When doing these in a tryout or practice situation, going a little slower but holding on to the ball is better than going as fast as possible with the ball bouncing off your foot across the gym floor every 10 seconds. You don't want coaches to see you chasing turnovers, you want them to see you holding on to the basketball.

- Around the waist, head, legs

Around the waist

Around the head

Around the legs

- Figure 8 dribble
- Blur
- Rhythm dribble
- Spider walk or dribble

(Handle the ball with your fingertips, not your palms. You will have better touch in your fingertips.)

Figure Eight Dribble: Use quick, little dribbles and make a figure eight: 1) right hand dribbles behind the right leg, 2) through the legs, switching to the left hand, 3) around left leg with the left hand, dribbling from front to back, 4) back through the legs switching to the right hand. 5) Do for 30 seconds and then reverse.

Blur: Start holding the ball between your legs (figure 1). Let go of the ball (figure 2). Switch your hands to the opposite position before the ball hits the ground. Go quickly and keep your head and eyes up.

Rhythm Dribble: Switching from your left to right hand, take two dribbles in front and then two dribbles in back. Left-right in front, left-right in back. Continue to follow this pattern. Start slowly and build your speed. Your dribbling should create a steady rhythm.

Spider Dribble: Dribble between your legs as you walk. With each step, the ball should travel between your legs from one hand to the other. The dribble should always travel from the front of your thighs, between your legs to the back of your thighs. This will keep the ball away from the defense. For the purpose of the drill, however, you may switch directions as you like. Do this drill a lot.

Station #2: Shooting Off The Pass

Shots, whether in practice drills or actual games, develop more from passing than they do from dribbling. The better the team, the more shots it shoots off the pass. Shooting off the pass without taking a dribble is extremely important to your success, because otherwise, you might not ever have a chance to shoot a high quality shot. Players don't want to pass up shots they can make, yet lots of players fail at being ready to shoot as they receive the ball, or even better, before they receive the ball. By the time they think about shooting, the shot is no longer open. Some players only feel comfortable if they can dribble first, making it impossible to shoot lots of outside shots with any consistency.

Stand facing the front of the basket about ten feet away. Spin the ball out so it comes back like a pass. Put your hands up in the shot pocket (the area starting from your chest going upwards where you actually hold the ball when getting ready to shoot) and step into the pass so that by the time the ball reaches your hands, your feet are already positioned for the shot (call this a one-two step). Every time you get ready to catch the ball and shoot it, your feet should take these two steps leaving you facing the basket ready to shoot by the time the ball arrives.

Get your hands and feet ready to shoot __before__ the ball arrives.

Rehearsing Shooting Off The Pass

Stand facing the basket at the right elbow of the free throw line. Have a friend stand under the basket with the ball. Have him or her pass it to you and shoot it from the right elbow. After shooting, run to the left elbow, facing the goal the entire time and shoot from the left elbow. Now back to the right elbow... and back. Shoot ten shots. The rebounder needs to do a good job of getting the ball quickly and passing it immediately to one of the shooting spots. Your footwork is the key – always step towards the pass and into the shot with your inside foot first. If facing the goal and moving to your left, then your right foot is the inside foot. If going to your right, your left foot is the inside foot (see photos on the following page).

Jason...Dream #1

I always have this dream...National
Championship game in some big
dome against some incredible team with
millions watching. Our starting point
guard is sidelined by a bad knee.
Five minutes into the first half,
his back-up goes down with
a sprained ankle. Following me so far?
Anyway, Coach tries to use our shooting
guard to bring the ball up court but
that just isn't getting the job done. With
about eight minutes left in the half, he looks down
the bench and mouths my name. I have no
doubt he's talking to me, mainly because I sit
at the very end of the bench and the only
person sitting past me is our manager,
and I doubt he is going to put him in the
game. I spring to my feet, grabbing at the
buttons of my warm-up jacket, and head to
the scorer's table as Coach barks a few
nervous instructions in my ear.

Station #3: Rebounding

Rebounding drills always turn into something closer to rugby than anything else. Usually it's three against three or five against five. The coach designates half the players as the defense and they line up as if they're guarding the others. The coach or a manager shoots the ball at the goal and everyone tries to rebound it. The emphasis is for the defense to block out, turning and putting a body on the offense to keep them from getting to the ball. While players are attempting to block out, there's a lot that goes on that no one talks about. No one ever mentions all of the holding and elbowing and jostling for position that occurs, much of which happens before the ball is ever shot. Don't get me wrong. Those people who block out well will rebound a lot more balls than those who don't. And those players who are taller and stronger and box out will snag even more

Carry your hands high, as if they are holding a ball, not at your sides.

rebounds. It's just that the players who stop at nothing, and I mean nothing, also get their fair share of boards. To the best of my knowledge, no one has ever been murdered in these drills. I'm not talking about causing dental damage or blindness nor am I suggesting karate chops to the knees. Really it's just a matter of expecting every shot to miss and that every one of these misses is your rebound no matter who might be trying to take it away.

Rebounding Drills

1. Practice tossing (underhanded) the ball off the back board with a friend or teammate standing behind you, working at not letting them come around you for the rebound. Make sure that the other person starts out leaning against your back or it's not really fair for the person throwing it off the backboard (figure 1). Each person go five or ten times, seeing who can get the most rebounds when throwing the ball off the glass (figure 2). With a bunch of friends, start off the same way but as long as the person who throws it up manages to get the rebound, he or she stays on until somebody gets around them and takes it.

Above: Figure 1
Right: Figure 2

2. While rebounding for a friend or teammate, see how many shots in a row (including makes) you can keep from hitting the ground. Sounds easy, I know, but see if you actually can keep the ball from hitting the ground. Almost every player in the gym will let the ball bounce to the ground before retrieving it. Be different. Whether it's this drill, a game,or you're just rebounding for someone else, try not to let the ball bounce. Show that you're serious about your game, even the little things. You don't have to be overly intense doing this, knocking everyone out of the way. Just try to never let the ball touch the ground. See how many shots in a row (including makes) you can keep off the floor.

Good rebounders expect every shot to miss.

Station #4: 3 On 3 Team Defense

Smaller games like 3 on 3 allow the coach to simplify more difficult concepts such as team defense. Since there are fewer people, it's a good opportunity for you to show off your defense.

The biggest challenge a player faces in playing team defense is going from an individual defense situation (pressuring an opponent with the ball) to a team defense situation (moving away from the opponent who doesn't have the ball to help guard an opponent who does.)

See both the person you're guarding and the ball. Use what's called peripheral vision to see both at the same time. Do this by pointing (actually point) at your opponent and the ball. Look straight ahead seeing the

ball out of one corner of your eye and your opponent out of the other corner. If you can't see both without turning your head, move backwards so they come into your view. This puts you in a position to help. Every time the ball moves on the pass or dribble away from the person you're guarding, you must anticipate where it's going and adjust your position so you can see the person you're guarding and the ball.

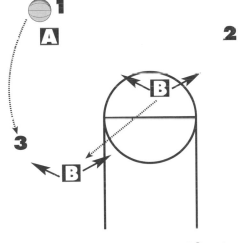

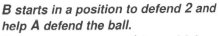

B starts in a position to defend 2 and help A defend the ball.
B then moves to stop 1 from driving.

Free Throws and Water

Even during breaks, see if you can be doing something positive. Everyone will rush for the water. Be different. Stay on the court and shoot free throws. You'll have a chance for some water when everyone else comes back.

Free Throw Technique

The best free throw shooters in the league, state, and nation achieve this status because they shoot more free throws than anyone around. Period. The reason they make pressure free throws isn't because they say special things to themselves or go through some magic routine, but because they feel comfortable on the line due to all the practice they've put in. No matter what anyone says, good free throw shooters are good free throw shooters because they shoot lots and lots and lots of free throws. By the way, it's this way with everything else as well; good dribblers dribble a lot, good shooters shoot a lot, and so on.

Right: Good free throw shooters shoot lots and lots and lots of free throws.

Jason's Basketball Diary

No one understands how important this is
to me. They say things like, "just try your
hardest, that's all you can do" but they just don't
get it. I want this more than anything in the
world. If I simply stopped playing because the coach
cut me, where would I be now? At what point in
my life would I have followed through on my goals?
Tryouts were so discouraging last year. There
was never any time to show what I could do. We just
drifted from one drill to the next, unsure of
exactly what was going on. And those games…
no one passed the rock and everyone kept dribbling
around turning it over. At least this year I
know what to expect. I'll probably know most of
the drills ahead of time so I'll know where I
have to be and what I'll have to do. I am going to
go after it harder than last year. I was frustrated and
just shuffled around trying to act cool. Forget
that. Coach better be ready 'cause I'm prepared
to do anything to make this happen. I've worked harder
than everyone all summer long. People I play
with tell me all the time how much better I've
gotten. I handle the ball much better than I did at
the beginning of the summer and my jump shot
has gotten awfully sweet. I must have gotten
better on defense because everyone yells at
me when I guard them. All those times in the weight
room by myself, the only one shooting jumpers
or showing up to play – I've improved,
I know I have.

Scrimmaging

Scrimmaging is the most misunderstood part of tryouts and practices. Everyone has dreams of shooting and scoring their way to spots on the team, yet this seldom happens. First of all, every player on the court also has visions of scoring points, making it less likely you'll get passed the ball when you're open for a shot. Secondly, coaches typically stop scrimmages in practice to make coaching points, which makes getting into any kind of flow very difficult. This all leads to an even bigger problem. Players end up getting so frustrated at not scoring that they start making lots of careless mistakes that doom their chances even more.

Develop realistic expectations of how you're going to play in scrimmages. It's all right to dream about nailing threes and driving to the hole, but more thought needs to be focused on what happens when you aren't scoring like a maniac. Otherwise, if your success is dependent on scoring a lot of points, you're likely to be disappointed more often than you'd like.

When scrimmaging, you need to be...
...in the RIGHT PLACE,
...at the RIGHT TIME,
...doing the RIGHT THING.

Go Get The Ball!

Nothing will get a player noticed more than when they hold the basketball in their hands. Coaches may talk a lot about recognizing hustle and good defense, but they see nothing as clearly as the player holding the ball. Yet, simply trying to catch the ball can be as frustrating as trying to score, as anyone who has ever played with ball hogs will confirm. Whether from good defense, picking up loose balls, rebounding or running hard on fast breaks, there are many different ways to gain possession of the ball and you must become aware of all of them.

Defense

Know and remember who you're guarding. You'd think I'd offer something more complicated considering all the skills it takes to play defense, yet this is the one that players screw up the most. "I have number 45." Say it so everyone hears you. "Who has number 25?" Communicate with your teammates to make sure everyone is picked up.

Loose Balls

My friend Mike Norwood, I swear, though it's not widely known, is the best basketball player of all time at getting his hands on loose balls. Mike can walk onto a court anywhere with anybody and be guaranteed he'll pick up two or three loose balls. He might not always score a lot or be the best player there, but when his team is down by a basket and on defense and the ball starts rolling around, Mike is always, always the one who gets it.

Rebound

They call professional basketball player Dennis Rodman "The Worm." He never shoots. He never scores. He misses practices. He only shows up right before game time, missing warm-ups completely. He gets fined routinely for flagrant fouls or run-ins with referees, other players, and fans. He even dyes his hair blue or yellow, depending on the opponent. Why, you may ask, is this guy still in the NBA? Well for starters, he averages near-ly 20 rebounds a game.

Take a Charge

Not only can you make the team by taking a few charges but your coach might remove your jersey there on the spot and hang it in the rafters as a tribute. Helping your teammates on defense creates lots of opportunities for stepping in front of an out-of-control player, getting your feet set and looking them in the numbers.

Right: Taking a charge... beat the offense to the spot.

Lower left: You must have both feet set with your arms to the side before contact, or it will be a blocking foul.

Lower right: Look directly into the chest of the offense and take a charge.

Run Hard

One way to stand out from the pack is to run ahead of it. That is, if you run down the court faster than everyone else, not only will you be alone and easy to see, but you're very likely to catch the ball since you'll probably be wide open. Getting ahead of the ball is more a matter of trying to outrun everyone else more than it is actually having world-class speed. Try to see how many players, whether on your team or the other, you can pass as you run down the court. You'll find you can pass even the fastest runners since most players seldom think in terms of outrunning anyone. Coaches will recognize this as an athletic play even though it's as much a product of your head as your running ability.

Line Up and Call For It

Line up and call for the ball. Running around like some crazed lunatic doesn't help get the ball, yet this is what many players end up doing. Learn to move with a purpose in mind. Use what's called a v-cut to get open. Try going to one spot, say the block down low on the lane. When you think the ball is getting good and close, walk a couple of steps towards the defender and then explode towards the ball. Clap your hands together one time and say the ball-handler's name out loud. This way you're easier to find because you aren't running around all over the place and your teammates will know you're much more serious about catching the ball because you're calling their name. Don't whine, though. Everyone hates to play with someone always saying, "Hey, throw it to me, everybody."

"Thanks"

Always, always thank teammates for helping you, especially for throwing you a good pass or an assist. Point to them, yell their name, hit them on the back or pat 'em on the fanny but always thank them or why else would they ever want to help you again.

Look It Into Your Hands

Catching might sound stupid to talk about, yet ball after ball sails through the buttery fingers of players everywhere. Some players drop passes so often that teammates stop throwing the ball to them. There isn't a specific drill that helps as much as simply concentrating on catching each time a pass is thrown your way. Make a big effort to be one of those players your teammates can always count on to catch the ball.

Screening

If you aren't catching the ball, help your teammates catch it. Screening is a great move because it shows you understand the game and are unselfish towards helping your teammates get open. Also, it gives you something to do when you don't have the ball. When you can't catch the ball, you can always go set a screen. Screening involves using your body to shield a teammate's defender

The screener
moves towards
the defender
guarding his
teammate.

The screener comes
to a comfortable
stop with his arms
down at his sides,
careful not to
charge into the
defender for a foul.
His teammate fakes
right...

... and uses the
screen by going left,
brushing against the
screener's right
shoulder, making it
impossible for the
defender to follow.

so your teammate can get free but the defender can't follow. When screening, come to a complete stop. Don't keep moving or it's called an illegal screen. Also, keep your arms down, not up. You can keep them in front of you for protection as long as they're straight down. If they're up, you'll be called for blocking.

Back Screens... A Great Move For Getting The Ball

Back screens are more fun than other screens because they not only free a teammate, but they help you catch the ball. Most screens consist of a player starting from the outside (away from the basket) and moving towards the inside or towards the basket to set a screen for a teammate. This frees your teammate on the outside but leaves you in a bunch of traffic unable to catch the ball. Back screens free your teammate to run towards the basket by you moving away from the basket and setting a screen on

Down Screen: A sets a screen on 1, allowing B to move unguarded towards the ball.

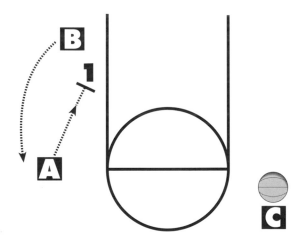

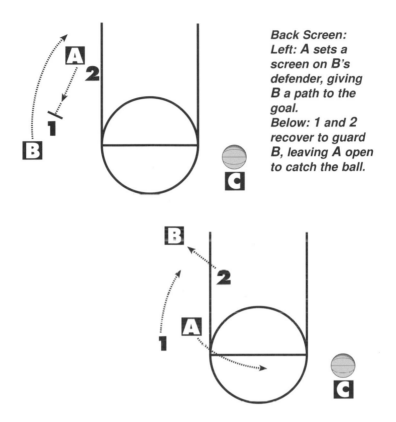

Back Screen:
Left: *A sets a screen on B's defender, giving B a path to the goal.*
Below: *1 and 2 recover to guard B, leaving A open to catch the ball.*

the perimeter. If the ball isn't thrown to your teammate, then you're in a great position to catch the ball since you're on the outside of the court instead of buried on the inside.

Make sure to call out your teammate's name, "This way, Andre," so they know to use the screen. If they don't use it, keep talking to them, "C'mon Andre, use the back screen so you can get the ball." Remember: set the back screen and then step towards the ball. You'll be surprised how many times you can catch it.

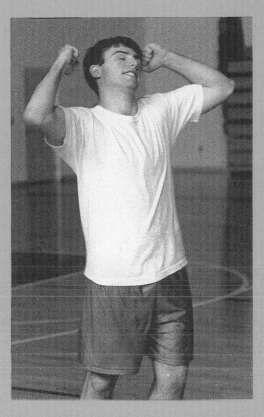

Jason...Scrimmaging

During the scrimmage, Jason becomes very
frustrated that he never gets to touch the ball.
Each time he gets open for a shot, one of
three things happens: 1) Someone shoots.
2) Someone turns the ball over. 3) The coach
stops the game to talk about something. To make
matters worse, the coach gets on his squad for not
playing good defense and singles out Jason for
being away from his defensive assignment. Jason
thinks the coach is wrong because he was
helping out his teammate who got
beaten on the play.

When You Get The Ball... Make The Easy Play

Lots of players have dreams about scoring countless buckets with incredible moves. Yet when the time comes to play, they don't even get a chance to catch the ball, or if they do, the ball gets slapped out of their hands.

Keep your expectations about how well you play in try-outs and practice simple. It's easier to have fun and play better if you don't try to win a championship every time you catch the ball. Concentrate on the simple things: Make strong moves to catch the ball. Face the basket. Shoot the shots you practice. Make the first easy play. Pass to the first open player. Make these plays over and over again and you'll always be in the flow of the game. This is the foundation from which you build the rest of your skills.

"A kid who doesn't throw the ball away and a kid who doesn't take bad shots is a pretty good player."

– Bobby Knight

Make The Easy Play – Face The Basket

Every time you catch the ball, no matter what the situation, you must turn and face the basket. Since you can't dribble, pass, or shoot without facing the goal (after all, you need the goal to score), it makes sense to learn how to face it first.

Turning without traveling is the most important step. Stand on the free-throw line with your back to the basket. Spin the ball out in front of you so it comes back like a pass. As you meet the ball, notice which foot is first to touch the ground when you catch it. This foot is your pivot foot. It must stay on the ground as you turn with the other foot or it will be traveling. Many players make the mistake of turning with their pivot foot, which is also traveling.

Technical Stuff Coaches Love To Talk About...

Many coaches want you to use what's called a jump stop when catching the ball. This involves landing on both feet at the same time (sort of hopping) as you catch the ball. Jump stops allow you to turn either way since both feet touch simultaneously, making them both potential pivot feet. Some coaches also make a big deal about whether you perform an inside turn or an outside turn.

- For inside turns, the non-pivot foot opens up and actually swings in towards the basket.
- For outside turns, the non-pivot foot swings around away from the basket (towards the outside).

Footwork for outside pivot turns   *Footwork for inside pivot turns*

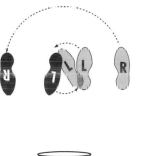

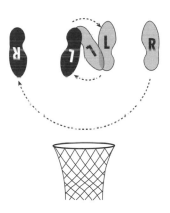

As you'll see with experience, you'll usually pivot toward the outside because it's a more natural motion from which to shoot. But in any case, don't worry so much about which turn you use as much as just turning, period.

Drill: Turning Against Pressure

Playing against pressure is one of the most useful talents you can develop, and pivoting is a major part of it. While standing on the free throw line with your back to the basket, have a friend stand directly behind you. As you spin the ball out and catch it, have your friend apply lots of physical pressure making it hard for you to turn. Don't dribble on this little sequence. The defense doesn't need to worry

Below: The defender applies lots of pressure, making it hard for the ball-handler to turn.

Above: Pivoting on his left foot, the ball-handler bends his knees and turns against the pressure.

Below:Having completed his turn, the ball-handler is ready to pass the ball or drive past the defender. Notice how well the ball is protected.

about getting beaten. The defense should slap the ball out of your hand if possible to get you in the habit of protecting it. Unless you have your knees bent and are anticipating turning against lots of physical contact, it's almost impossible to face the basket, let alone shoot, pass or dribble the ball. Practice turning against the defense with this kind of intensity and you'll be surprised how much easier it is to play against a really tough defense.

Protect The Ball

One of the most frustrating experiences in basketball is having the ball slapped or grabbed out of your hands. Just thinking about protecting the ball is half the battle. Stand toe to toe, face to face with someone. With the ball in your hands, have the other person try to knock the ball free. By not moving your feet or pivoting in this drill, you'll get used to protecting the ball. Bend your knees plenty. Take the ball from one side to the other, experimenting with different ways to protect the ball and keep it away from the defender.

Passing It To Yourself

Learning this little flick of the wrists is important because it allows you to practice your skills as if you are catching a pass without actually having someone throw you the ball. Simply hold the ball in both hands and toss it out in front of you with plenty of back spin so the ball comes right back as you go to meet it. By tossing it out a little higher or farther, you can make the ball meet you at different spots.

Make The Easy Play – Now Or Never

To shoot or not to shoot doesn't need to be a gut-wrenching decision. Take the guess work out of it. Either shoot the ball immediately when you get it, whether it's an outside shot or a drive, or don't at all. **IF YOU FEEL TWO POINTS, STAND UP AND SHOOT IT.** In order to make any strong offensive move, you've got to know ahead of time what you're going to do. For example, if the defense is way off and you're wide open for a shot, you must get your feet and hands and body ready to shoot before the ball arrives to keep you from hesitating once you get it. Players who hold the ball while deciding what to do next have little chance of putting the ball in the hole and an even greater chance of making a mistake. The longer they hold it, the more time the defense has to adjust which makes scoring difficult and turnovers likely.

Also, only shoot shots with which you're most comfortable. These shots are the ones you shoot over and over again in practice. Shooting a shot just because it's the first open one you've had all day, even though it's five feet outside your range, is not the sign of a great shooter. Shots that are strong, comfortable, open and within your range make you look good. Shots that are hurried, forced and outside of your range make you look unsure and inexperienced.

Make The Easy Play – Pass The Rock

1. Pass to the first open player you see the instant you see one. Don't wait. Don't hold it. Give up the rock. Most players hold the ball too much and don't pass enough.

2. Dropped passes are the passer's responsibility, not the receiver's. Throw all your passes with this little rule in mind and you'll probably think twice about throwing that bullet no one can catch.

3. Be accurate with your passes. Aim for a specific target, not just somewhere near where you're trying to throw it. Magic Johnson reportedly aims for the face on his passes, figuring most people don't miss passes thrown at their face.

4. Step through with your feet when you pass the ball, the same way a quarterback steps with one foot to put something on the ball. Flat-footed passes have nothing on them and are easy for the defense to steal.

These passes are easy to learn but remember, it's the results that count – completed passes!

Chest Pass

Place two hands on each side of the ball with the ball under your chin. Step forward on one foot and extend both arms, pushing through the ball. Follow through with your palms facing outward. The ball should have a nice easy backspin when thrown. Just for learning's sake, try throwing this pass without using your thumbs to get the proper feel and spin.

Outlet or Overhand Pass

Using your legs by stepping in the direction of the pass is the key to this one. Put the ball high over your head with your hands on each side of the ball. Without bringing the ball down or bringing it behind your neck,

Left and below:
Chest Pass

Above and right: Outlet or
Overhand Pass

Left and below: Bent-Elbow Pass

*Above and right:
Bounce Pass*

step forward and extend your arms forward, keeping them high as you follow through. Really try to put some zing on this pass. Your hands will follow through a lot like a chest pass with your palms turning outward, though they won't turn as much since your hands are up higher.

Bent-Elbow Pass

Former Duke Academic All-American Dick DiVenzio makes a case for this one in his excellent basketball book, *STUFF*. This pass is extremely versatile and can be used at any time. Tuck your right elbow against your side. Bringing the ball to the right side with both hands, extend your right hand through the ball, pushing in the direction you wish to pass, following through with your right hand towards the target. Just reverse these instructions for throwing the ball left-handed.

Bounce Pass

This is simply a chest or bent-elbow pass thrown at the ground. Aim two-thirds of the way between you and your target. The ball should bounce up above the receiver's waist. Bounce passes are excellent for throwing on fast breaks when the person you're throwing to has a lay-up. Also, throwing a bounce pass bent-elbow style makes it much easier to hit a player posting up on the inside.

Jason...Dream #2

This dream is actually more like a
nightmare. I'm always late,
walking into the locker room
while everyone else is walking
out onto the court already dressed
in their uniforms. I hurry to
get dressed but I can't find
my locker and discover I don't
have one. The managers all look
at me as if I don't belong
there but I finally talk one
of them into giving me a
uniform. By the time I get out
on the floor, warm-ups
are almost over and
everyone just looks at me
like I'm some kind of idiot.

TALKING

"Let's run."
"Keep it moving."
"Switch."
"I have number 33."
"Help!"
"Watch the screen."
"Nice pass."
"Good defense."
"Way to run."
"I have the basket."
I have the ball."
"Yeah!"
"Block 'em out."

Basketball demands communication. Passing isn't the only way to show teamwork. Show your personality. Think the game outloud. Appreciate a good play. Take the blame for a mistake everyone knows someone else really committed. Exhibit some leadership. Motivate others. Certain plays require talking, such as warning a teammate about a screen or letting the ball-handler know someone is behind trying to steal the ball. The basketball court is no place for shyness. It's your court as much as any one else's so open your mouth and let everyone know you're serious about playing.

Make The Easy Play – Take It To The Hoop

Driving the ball well takes a lot of practice but it's also one of the most fun plays you can make. Many players aren't good drivers because they have poor footwork. They never turn and face the basket and the defense, which makes getting by the defense difficult. When most players try to drive against pressure, they end up rushing, which results in shuffling feet and traveling calls. Imagine what must be going through a coach's mind when they see the same player travel every time he or she touches the ball. Probably something along the lines of, "I'd love to keep the kid on my team, but the competition is too close and this kid is an instant turnover."

"Be quick, but not in a hurry."

– John Wooden

Starting

Stand on the free throw line with your back to the basket. Spin the ball out, catch it, turn and face the basket. Once again, have a friend make it tough for you to turn and face the basket. Once you're able to turn and face, you probably don't want to stand there and let this person beat on you, so what you need to do is: (1) keep your pivot foot planted (keep it planted!), (2) step out with your non-pivot foot, trying to get your head and shoulders past the defender (3) and explode by the defense, making sure to dribble the ball before lifting your back pivot foot (see example on following page). Your dribble should be nice and low to keep it away from the defense. The defender doesn't need to follow your drive. Keep going to the basket and shoot a lay-up.

Keep your foot planted, step out with your non-pivot foot, trying to get your head and shoulders past the defensive person and explode by the defense, making sure to dribble the ball before lifting your back pivot foot.

The Dribbling Dilemma

Dribbling is quite a dilemma for players with something to prove. On one hand, you must be able to dribble comfortably and effectively. But on the other hand, there probably isn't another part of the game that gets players in as much trouble.

If you're going to dribble, think about using two dribbles or less. There's seldom ever a reason for dribbling more than this. In just two dribbles you can find an open teammate or take it to the hoop. You need to make each dribble count by covering as much ground as possible on each dribble. Too many players stand around dribbling without moving. These are just wasted dribbles. If you're going to dribble, you've got to go somewhere.

Dribbling Basics: 1) Keep your head up and see the entire floor. 2) Protect the ball with your non-dribbling hand. 3) Stay low to the ground.

Have An Offensive and Defensive Emphasis

There are tons of things you have to consider when playing, yet trying to remember everything may actually get in the way of playing your best. By concentrating on a couple of solid ideas – an offensive and defensive emphasis – you'll have a simple, yet effective game plan for keeping your concentration steady on both sides of the court. Here's an example:

> Offensive Emphasis – face the basket
> Defensive Emphasis – pressure the dribbler

When things feel chaotic or confusing, concentrate on your emphasis. It will quiet your mind and this will free your body to play hard and well.

Warning: You Might Only Scrimmage

It is highly possible that when you show up for tryouts, the coach will divide everyone into teams and have everyone play games. As we've talked about, scrimmaging can be a frustrating tryout situation. An entire practice of scrimmaging might just drive you nuts. Your ability to take advantage of every single moment becomes even more crucial because there may be even fewer chances to show what you can do. One advantage, though, is that you get to show how well you put all your skills together – play hard defense, dive for a steal, run hard to get ahead of the ball, make a nice assist for a lay-up and compliment your teammate for catching the ball.

Conditioning

During tryouts and practices, there will be some sort of running drills or defensive sliding drills or something that is designed to make players dead tired. These conditioning drills present a tremendous, TREMENDOUS chance for not only showing your athletic ability and endurance, but for also showing how badly you're willing to try in order to accomplish your goals. Even when your stomach hurts and your legs are tired and you feel like you're going to throw up, still give your all and try to beat everyone and come in first. Dive for second place. Pass your main competition. Try to beat someone who is faster.

**Out-of-shape short people usually have a
hard time making the team.**

Running???

Lots of players join cross country and track teams fantasizing that they'll score hundreds and hundreds of points playing basketball when everyone else is tired and worn out. If the coach really wants kids interested in basketball to run track, then do it. However, never forget: nothing will improve your endurance for playing basketball more than playing lots and lots of basketball. Play lots and lots of games. Make yourself run harder while everyone else is tired. Cross half court during every change of possession. Learn to overcome tiredness by making yourself worn out and then overcoming it.

If you absolutely feel that some sort of running will

better prepare you for the season, fine. Here's a good running program:

1. Start running
2. When you get tired, keep running.
3. When you absolutely can go no further, keep running.
4. Repeat the next day.

Jumping Rope

Jumping rope is excellent for basketball players. It develops quickness, coordination and endurance. Any piece of rope will do, though something with handles usually doesn't cost much and is easier on your hands. Make sure the rope is long enough. While standing with both feet on the center of the rope, the ends should come

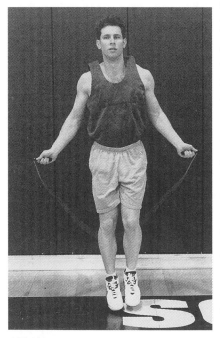

at least a foot above your waist. Start jumping on both legs. Eventually alternate from leg to leg. Try one leg at a time. Cross your hands back and forth (watch _Rocky II_ & _III_ for good jump roping moves). A clock on the wall or stop watch helps keep track of time. Listen to music if at all possible. It helps the time go by and improves your dancing.

Try these workouts:

Workout #1

  Quick

      Jump 1 minute
      Rest 1 minute
      Total 20 minutes
      (10 jumping/10 resting)

  Quicker

      Jump 1 minute
      Rest 30 seconds
      Total 21 minutes
      (14 jumping/7 resting)

  Quickest

      Jump 5 minutes
      Rest 1 minute
      Total 30 minutes
      (25 jumping/5 resting)

Workout #2

  Quick

      Jump 3 minutes
      Rest 1 minute
      Total 20 minutes
      (15 jumping/5 resting)

  Quicker

      Jump 1 minute/rest 1 minute
      Jump 2 minutes/rest 1 minute
      Jump 3 minutes/rest 1 minute
      Jump 4 minutes/rest 1 minute
      Jump 5 minutes/rest 1 minute

  Quickest

      Do the above workout and then
      jump your way down to 1 minute.

Workout #3

Quick	Jump 5 minutes
	Rest 1 minute
	Total 18 minutes
	(15 jumping/3 resting
Quicker	Jump 15 minutes straight
Quickest	Jump 30 minutes straight

Getting Strong

The following list of exercises may look basic but do not let it fool you. These are tremendous tools for developing strength in all of the main muscle groups, and with lots of work, you can experience significant gains in strength.

Push-ups: Everyone knows how to do this one yet most people fail to realize how tremendous this exercise is for developing upper body strength. Push-ups primarily develop the chest muscles (pectorals) with a secondary emphasis on the shoulder (deltoids) and rear arm (triceps) muscles. When doing this movement, make sure that your pelvis and chest are even. When going down, they should both touch the floor just slightly. Don't cheat by sticking your butt in the air or by not going all the way down to the floor. To work different areas, try placing your hands at different widths. A wide hand position emphasizes your chest and shoulders, while a narrow one emphasizes your triceps. Also try putting your feet on a chair while leaving your hands on the ground – this will hit your upper chest and shoulders. Advanced people can also do push-ups while doing a

handstand against the wall which also emphasizes the shoulders and triceps. Regardless of the style, do this exercise as many times in a row as possible until you can't do another one. Keep strict, proper form as your muscles get fatigued. Rest one minute and repeat two to four more times.

A sample routine might look like this: 40 push-ups, 1 minute rest, 35 push ups, 1 minute rest, 30 push-ups, 1 minute rest and 30 push-ups. Adjust the number higher or lower to match your ability but make sure you push yourself. If the last five repetitions of each set aren't killers, then you probably aren't doing enough repetitions.

Pull-ups: Another exercise that works several muscles at once. Pull-ups primarily develop the back muscles (Latissimus dorsi) which will give your back an athletic

V shape. There is also a secondary emphasis on the front arm (bicep) and forearm muscles. From a dead hang, pull yourself up to the bar by squeezing your back muscles. Don't swing or kick to give yourself momentum. Use a wide overhand grip with palms facing forward to emphasize your back muscles. Use a narrow underhanded grip, with the palms facing towards you for working your biceps. Try doing 50 repetitions. Unless you're an olympic gymnast, you'll have to break these into separate sets. Your sets may look like this: 10-9-7-7-5-5-3-2-2. Rest no longer than a minute between sets. If this is too hard, then pick a lower number of repetitions (30 or 40). Don't be discouraged if you can only do a few repetitions at a time. Be patient and use this exercise as a measuring stick. If you get after it with some intensity, you'll be able to see incredible improvement in not much time at all.

Lunges: A leg exercise that works the top of your thigh (quadricep), the back of your thigh (hamstring) and your rear end (gluteus). You can either do this one holding dumbbells at your side or a barbell across the back of your shoulders. You can also do this exercise without using any additional weights. Just put your hands on your hips and do more repetitions (at least 15-20). With your feet together, take a medium step directly forward. Leaving your back foot on the floor and your upper body straight up and down, drop your hips directly toward the floor. Go down until your front leg is almost parallel with the ground. To go back up, make sure you only use the strength in your front leg to push you upwards. Do

approximately 10-20 with each leg for 3-5 sets. Variation: Try walking the length of a gym while doing lunges. Go slowly and take consistent, medium steps. Step with the right foot, lunge and up. Step with the left foot, lunge and up. Continue. Consider each length of the court one set and do 3-5 of them.

Crunches: Working your stomach (abdominal) muscles is crucial. Since these muscles are the center of your body, they are involved in about any kind of movement. Strong abdominal muscles help make you faster, quicker and stronger as well as less susceptible to injury, especially in your lower back. Lie on your back with your knees bent and your feet flat on the ground. Tense your stomach muscles as tightly as possible. Flatten your lower back and spine against the ground to make sure you are using all of the little muscles. This is the feeling you should have the entire time you are doing crunches. Now put your hands behind your head but be careful not to pull on your neck. Your elbows should be directly out to the sides, your hands only acting as a pillow for your head. Pulling with your tightened stomach muscles, peel your shoulder blades off the ground slowly. Keep your eyes fixed towards the ceiling so you don't strain your neck. Go up as high as you can, tightening your stomach as much as you can stand. Even when you go back down, your abdominal muscles should remain flexed. For starters, try doing 20-30 of these with proper form. Do about 4-5 sets. Since you use your ab muscles everyday, they will only respond to constant daily attention. Take very little time in between sets, 20-30 seconds at most. Almost treat your stomach workout as one long set.

Listen to music while you do these and do them for an entire song without stopping. While watching TV, do them from one commercial break to another (not just for one commercial). Try these different types of crunches. Your hands will be behind your head for each one.

Bent-knee, feet flat: Works the entire abdominal muscle group, especially the lower muscles. As described above, keep your stomach tensed the entire time as your shoulders raise and lower.

Bent-knee, feet in the air: Works entire stomach, especially the upper muscles. Bring your knees and chest towards one another. (See photos below).

Knee-to-elbow: Concentrates on the side stomach muscles (obliques). With your knees bent and your feet in the air, bring your right elbow towards your left knee. Then bring your left elbow to your right knee. Repeat. Be careful not to pull on your neck.

How many times do I do each exercise? Each time you do one movement of a single exercise is called a repetition. For example, you might do 30 repetitions when doing push-ups. Each time you perform a given number of repetitions is called a set. You might do 4 sets of 30 push-ups for a total of 120 push-ups. You should not rest more than one minute between any given set. Resting too long gives your muscles too much time to recuperate. After all, you don't get much time to rest in the middle of a basketball game.

How often should I do these exercises? About every other day. Your muscles need about 24 hours to recuperate from strength training. Doing the same exercise and working the same muscles each day will only lead to injury and fewer results. You should, however, work your stomach muscles every day. Your stomach is made up of stubborn little muscles that you use in every day movements meaning that it takes a lot of hard work to make them strong.

The above exercises are only intended to get you started. Read books and magazines about weightlifting. Learn different types of exercises so you don't get bored with the same old workout. Make up your own workout routines. This way you can concentrate on your weaknesses, plus, it's usually more fun.

Read your body properly. If something isn't right, you should stop that particular exercise. But don't let up just because you don't like the uncomfortable feeling of trying to pull or push without anything happening.

Stretching

Everyone knows they should stretch some before and after playing but no one ever does. No one ever takes just a few seconds to loosen up by going up and down the court a few times. Bazillions of injuries occur year after year and nobody knows why.

Here are a few stretching exercises to get you started. Hold each stretch for approximately 15 seconds.

Left: Stretch your hands high into the air. Hold for awhile, until it feels good.
Right: Let yourself drop slowly into a hang. Keep your legs straight but stay relaxed.

Above: Lunge to one side, hold for 15 seconds and repeat to the other side.

Above: Stretch your groin by crouching with your heels relatively close together. Use your elbows to press your knees outward.

With your toes pointing forward, stretch your calf muscle by putting one leg in front of the other. Keep the back heel flat on the ground and the back leg straight.

Stretch your achilles, the tendon just above your heel, by doing the previous exercise but slightly bending the back knee towards the floor while keeping the heel flat

Gently pull your leg behind you. Repeat on the other leg.

Improving Jumping Ability

Coaches tell you that how high you jump really doesn't determine how good of a basketball player you are, yet all we see on T.V. are college and professional players who can jump out of the gym. Jumping alone will not get you on the team. It's much better to be a good shooter or ball-handler or defender. However, there is nothing wrong with working on your jumping. It helps get you into good basketball shape, and plus, jumping is fun.

Nothing will improve your leaping ability more than simply jumping a lot. Forget the special exercises, shoes, and other gimmicks. Just jump, jump, jump... I remember one summer doing nothing but shooting jump shots day after day. Each day while I was shooting, a teammate of mine who lived in the neighborhood would walk up the street to a low goal so he could learn how to dunk. The goal was just low enough to where he could put it through but he had to work at it. Once it became easy, he'd find another goal slightly higher. This continued all summer. By the time basketball season came around, I had become a pretty decent shooter and he could dunk on a regulation goal with no problem. Later, he became a spectacular leaper known for his soaring dunks. Whatever you do though, don't use trampolines or ramps or ladders to propel yourself for a dunk. This has more to do with being a stunt man than a basketball player. It's hard to make the team with a broken leg.

Injuries...

How someone responds to unfortunate circumstances often tells more about that person's character than when things are all peachy. If doctors in America had their way, every time a player fell down or sprained an ankle, an ambulance would whisk that player away to the hospital for x-rays, tests, casts and two months rest. But the fact of the matter is there are few injuries from which a player can't bounce back. Extremely few. Usually the serious ones involve blood, swelling, cracking noises, abnormal heart beats or some real obvious sign that things are not well.

What I'm talking about are the injuries where the player runs into another player, falls down, rolls around, lies there for three minutes, limps off and is ready to come back in five minutes. You know what

I'm talking about, it happens at least every other day, if not every time you play. Exactly what illness has symptoms that make you paralyzed for three minutes, but then goes away so you can make a heroic return to play? Yeah, right. Bounce up when you get shaken up a little. The pain will probably go away if you want it to.

Remarks

Usually at the end of a practice, coaches like to talk a bit about whatever is on their minds. Whenever coaches speak to the group, get up front where you can see and hear them. Make eye contact. Nod to show that you understand the instructions and you're not asleep.

"During the last two months of the summer of 1948, I really stepped up my basketball program. The whole family looked forward to having me on the varsity basketball team. The words of the JV coach were still fresh in my mind, but what kept me going even more than that was the fact that he had taken the time to encourage me. He believed in me, and that made me believe in myself.

I didn't go out for football or any other fall sport because fall was such a busy time on the farm. I slept well every night, exhausted after a day at school, hours in the fields, and more hours playing basketball. I was happy. I looked forward to making the varsity. It was a great experience for me and helped me later when I could remember how important it was to me to make the team. I am always very careful in choosing my teams, taking into account the number of guys who would give anything to make it.

The football season ended and basketball tryouts were announced. I had improved on my skills and endurance and I figured I'd have a good shot at a varsity job.

Several guys were there, so the coach told us that there would be three cuts to trim the team to size. Everyone would be given a fair shot and a good look.

For the first week or so I was doing fine. Everything was working for me, and I was even shooting better. I moved well without the ball too and hoped I was impressing the coach. I survived the first two cuts, and I felt I was going to make it.

The coach was initiating a new program. The varsity hadn't done too well in the recent past, and as a new coach, he wanted to shake things up a bit and try to turn things around. I was catching on quickly to his new program, and there didn't seem to be a lot of good players available. I think he knew early that it was going to be a difficult year. Certainly there were no superstars to build a team around. I hoped we would gel and be able to hustle ourselves into prominence for the coach.

There were just a few days left before the final cut. I didn't want to take any chances. I couldn't let up. I played with abandon, even going for rebounds against the bigger kids I'd been doing it for several days, showing the coach that I was willing to tussle with anyone to cement a spot on the team.

Then it happened. I raced through the lane and leaped for an offensive rebound. I was bumped on the way down and twisted my left ankle. When I hit the ground I knew it was bad. Pain shot up my leg to my knee. Even my toes hurt.

I discovered later that I had chipped some bones besides ripping some tendons and muscles, but back then you didn't just run to the doctor and have something x-rayed every time you got hurt. My leg was black and blue from my instep to my calf. It was excruciating, but I had it wrapped and hobbled around, anxious for the mobility to return so I wouldn't have to sit on the bench too long.

I watched practice for the next couple of days. Then the coach posted the names of the players who were to remain on the team after the final cut.

My name wasn't there. I quickly read the list again. My chest was cold. A coach can make mistakes in judging talent, but he'll never make a mistake in posting the final list. I would realize later that three other seniors had been cut too, but right then I was thinking of no one but me. I stood staring at the list. I couldn't move. I couldn't even talk. Guys were crowding around the list asking who made it and who didn't. I looked straight ahead and went to wait an hour for the bus.

I tried to tell myself it was because of my ankle. I think I could have helped the team, but now I had no chance. I hated the coach. I hated school. I hated everything. I was so ashamed, so embarrassed. I don't know what it's like to lose a member of my family, but I can't imagine feeling any worse than I felt that day. After all the work I had put in, now I had been left out.

The bus dropped me off about four blocks from home. I didn't really want to go home, but there was nowhere else to go. I didn't have to say anything. My parents knew I hadn't made it by the way I walked in. It was a sad day for them, too. That night I walked out by the pole where the backboard hung. I stood there with my hands thrust deep into the pockets of my Levis. Winter was near and a cold wind whipped around my *neck.*

I had worked so hard, so long. I had done everything I could have done. Basketball was the one oasis from the classroom and the hard work on the farm. What was there to look forward to now?"

– "Cut," from *Stuff It*
by Dick Motta

What would you do?

You've just worked your butt off for an entire summer or longer, yet, when you stare at that infamous list, your name is missing.

More people than not who have aspired to play basketball have found themselves in this exact situation – freshly cut from the school basketball team. With each person, a different story has resulted. Some players never touch a basketball again and some make the team the very next year. Some become disinterested in school and most everything else while others go on to become artists, senators and astronauts. Some learn nothing from the experience except disappointment, while others use the experience to propel them towards more satisfaction than they might have ever dreamed. **You can not determine everything about your situation or what happens to you, but you do decide what happens next.** You decide your next course of action. Overall, you couldn't ask for a better option.

Goals

"Goals. Some are realistic. Some
aren't. You gotta bust your butt to
find out. One thing's for sure, life
preys on one-dimensional
players, those who put
everything in one basket. It's
not fair. But you realize, it's
not your ball. So you've set
many goals. Earn a Ph.D.
Finish a marathon.
Write a screenplay.
Own an N.F.L. team.
Run for President.
Yeah, you're shooting for the
stars. But that's cool. If you don't
make one, you take what
you learned and alter your shot.
Just do it."

Advertisement from NIKE

CHAPTER THREE

GETTING READY

So you've just finished reading this book? You've analyzed your situation in the first section and learned more about what it takes to become a player in the second section. Now what? Tryouts don't start until November 1st and it's not even summer yet. What's the first step?

Simple. Grab your ball and head to the gym or driveway or playground. Stay a long time. Do it again tomorrow and the next day. **You will not become the player you want to be overnight but you can improve each day and take consistent steps toward your goals.**

Individual Practice

To get significantly better, playing pick-up games is not enough. You must spend time by yourself or with a friend working on your skills. Work on the weakest parts of your game every day or they'll always hold you back and never become strengths. How long should you practice? There isn't any magical time limit that, once surpassed, will turn you into Magic, Larry or Michael. Just remember that you're practicing a competitive sport and that means you're not alone. Others are practicing too. Practicing to beat you.

Competition

Competition, whether it's in a summer league or pick-up games, is great because it provides the perfect opportunity for testing the skills you practice by yourself. However, you can't practice your good habits one day and forget about them the next. You can't afford to be one of the players who never gets back on defense or always turns the ball over trying crazy plays. Practice your skills whenever you step on a court. Shoot the shots you'd shoot in real games. See if you can always be ahead of the ball no matter if you're going to defense or to offense.

Pick-up games are important even though no one really watches them and the results don't appear in the paper. Can you imagine what your coach would say if you only ran back on defense part of the time?

Set an emphasis each time you play – something you

really want to work on. For example, try guarding the ball-handler the entire length of the court. Pick him or her up the minute he or she touches the ball and get good at applying pressure.

Play with older and better players. It not only makes you tougher, but by playing against players who are stronger and quicker, you'll become stronger and quicker as you try to keep up.

If you regularly play on a court or playground where people tend to hog the ball and don't pass it when you're open, try showing up with or meeting a couple of friends at a designated time. This way you can play on a team with people more likely to pass the rock.

Off-Season Conditioning

Many coaches put their teams through conditioning and weight lifting programs in the off season. Besides the obvious hope of turning weaker players into stronger ones, coaches figure players need something that will keep them in shape.

If the school team has an off-season or preseason conditioning program, you need to find out about it and use it to your advantage. Even if the program is only available to kids who played last year, work out a deal with the coach. If the coach won't let you participate, ask him or her for a copy of the workout so you can do it on your own.

Consider the weights or running as another practice drill such as rebounding or defensive drills. Approach it the same way. Show up to the weight room first. Make your improvement the most drastic when compared to everyone else's. While other players take this off-the-court training less seriously, you'll have an excellent chance to show how dedicated you are towards becoming a valuable part of the team.

Even if there isn't a structured conditioning program set up, you need to develop your own. Focus on the parts of your physical conditioning that you want to improve and use the suggestions from the previous section to improve these areas.

But remember, as we discussed in the skill section with regard to conditioning, nothing will prepare and train your body for playing good basketball more than playing lots and lots of basketball.

DATE	TOTAL TIME	GAMES & DRILLS	
MON			
TUES			
WED			
THURS			
FRI			
SAT			
SUN			

Total Time This Week:

This Week I Improved:

	WHAT I WORKED ON	TOMMORROW'S PLAN

Total Time Last Week:

Next Week's Plan:

DATE	TOTAL TIME	GAMES & DRILLS	
MON	2:30 hrs.	*Full-court games at the Rec center...* *Shot 100 freethrows.*	
TUES	3:00 hrs.	*Weights after school* *Driveway & jumpshots off pass & dribble.* *One-on-one with Steve*	
WED	2:00 hrs.	*Full-court / Rec center* *Never lost!!*	
THURS	2:45 hrs.	*Weights after school* *Shot at school, made 39 freethrows in a row.*	
FRI	3:15 hrs.	*Games at Rec* *Jumped rope in driveway & shot.*	
SAT	3:30 hrs.	*Played outdoors at the park and dunked on a low goal at the elementary school.*	
SUN	2:00 hrs.	*Shot in driveway & did ball-handling drills.*	

Total Time This Week: *19 hrs.*

This Week I Improved: *Getting my feet ready to shoo before the pass arrives.*

WHAT I WORKED ON	TOMORROW'S PLAN
Tried to get ahead of the ball by running hard. Got some easy baskets.	*Need to be tougher when handling the ball in traffic.*
Worked on footwork when getting ready to shoot.	*Need to be ready to shoot when open from the outside.*
Hit lots of jumpers. Guarded Marvin & Ricky well, couldn't score on me.	*Turned the ball over too many times when driving. Need to keep head up.*
Still trying to get my feet ready before I shoot.	*Jump rope and work on quickness.*
Shot well, but turned the ball over too much.	*Spend more time with the basketball – dribbling and ball-handling.*
Surprised myself with my jumping ability – I got up as well as anyone.	*Still need to work on ball-handling more.*
Ball-handling: keeping my head up & using my left hand.	*More ball-handling & some jump rope.*

Total Time Last Week: *17.5 hrs*

Next Week's Plan: *Take the ball everywhere I go Really need to improve dribbling. Dunking on low goals is fun and is making my legs strong.*

What Happens to Jason?

Well, Jason made the team and
found out that being on the team
can be even more frustrating than
getting cut. It was hard
understanding exactly what the
coach wanted and expected.
As a result, Jason didn't get
to play a whole lot. Each day
in practice Jason found another
aspect of his game he needed to improve.

Though the season eventually
drew to a close, Jason found his
season just starting. He
signed up for some other leagues.
When he wasn't playing there,
he went to the local college
rec center and played against
older players. Every day,
he worked by himself on specific
skills and then tested the results

later in the day when playing
against others. Each afternoon,
he worked out religiously
on weights, quickness drills
and dunking on a low goal
in the neighborhood. Playing
against competition became more
and more enjoyable as
he experienced the results
of his hard work. The high
point came at the end
of the summer when he was playing
in a summer league game
with most of the kids who
played on the team last year.
With the team's coach
watching from the stands,
Jason played great. He guarded
the team's best player
from the year before and
forced him into a bad
shooting performance.
He even made a steal

near the end that helped
his team go on to win the game.
The coach told Jason
afterwards that he hadn't had
a player in a long time
who had improved as much
over the summer. This
made Jason work even harder
as tryouts drew nearer.
There were still many
areas in which he needed to
improve but this actually
made him excited;
excited because he knew
now that his success was
determined by him as much
as anything else.

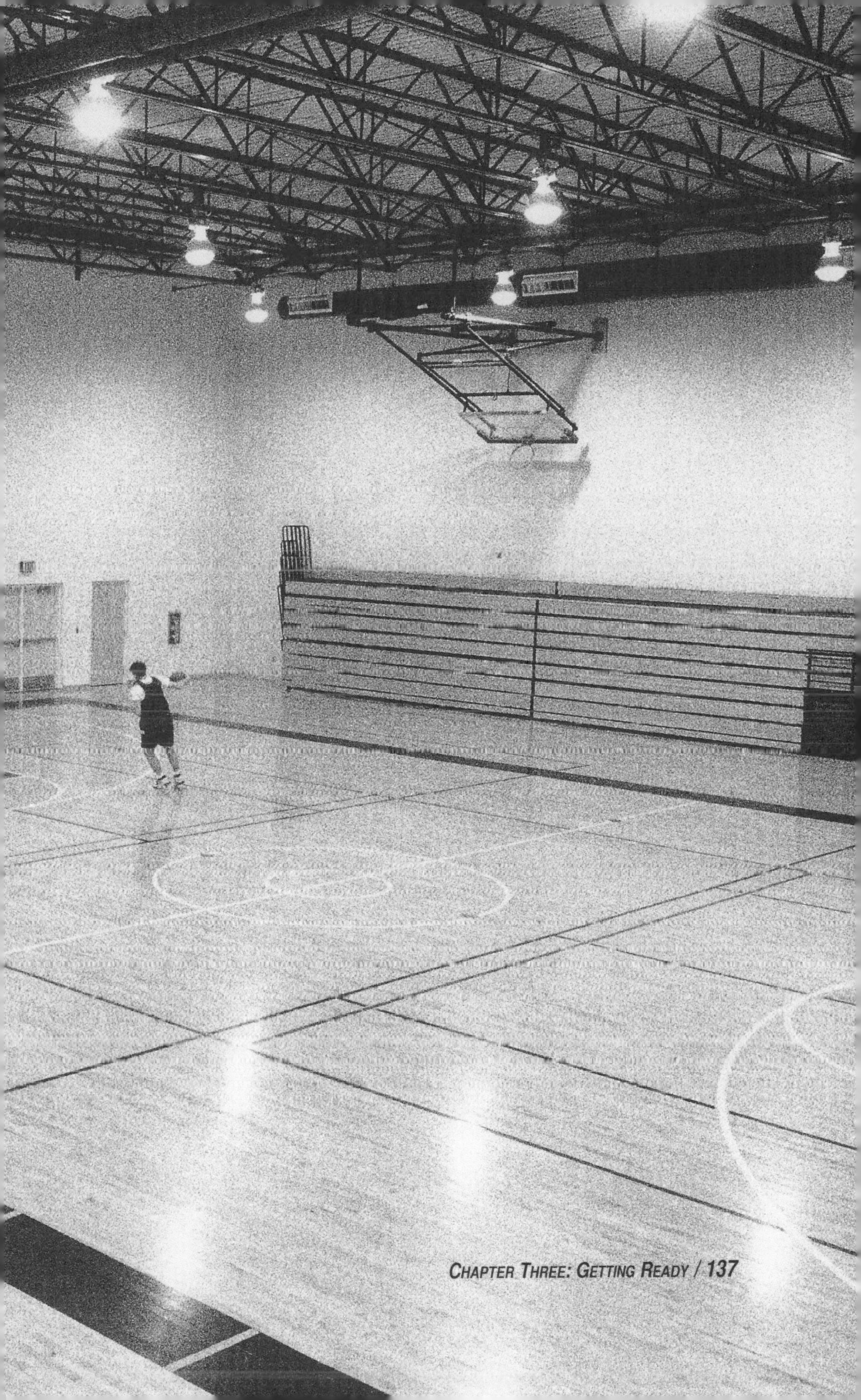

About the Author

Lane Czaplinski is the author of *Making The Basketball Team: Get Off The Bench And Into The Game;* a skills manual for young men and women trying to play competitive basketball. As the son of a longtime basketball coach, Lane grew up playing the game with a steady framework for developing his skills. While he never became Michael Jordan or Magic Johnson, the skills he developed over a number of years enabled him to enjoy an exciting career at each level, culminating in a slot on one of the country's best programs, The University of Kansas men's basketball team. As co-captain of the '91,92 Jayhawks, Lane was a part of a Big Eight championship, Big Eight post-season championship, and a NCAA tourney berth. Since graduating from Kansas University, Lane has coached a men's and women's high school basketball team in Hawaii and 5th through 12th graders each summer at the Roy Williams Basketball Camp in Lawrence, Kansas.

Index

Ball-Handling
Dribbling, 101
Drills, 57-62

Conditioning
During Practice, 103
Injuries, 117-118
Jumping Ability, 116-117
Jumping Rope, 104-106
Off-Season, 126-127
Running, 103-104
Strength Exercises, 106-113
Stretching, 113-116
Warming Up, 30

Defense
Defensive Emphasis, 102
Denying, 56
Fouling, 56
Full-Court, Bump & Run, 54-55
Know Who You're Guarding, 77
Loose Balls, 77
One-On-One, 49-51
Quick Slides, 48
Step-Slides, 46-48

Sliding, 45
Taking A Charge, 44,78
Team Defense, 70-71

Fastbreak
Defending, 44
Drill, 39-40
Situations, 40-41

Jason, 26-27, 32-33, 42-43, 52-53,
66 67, 74 75, 84-85, 96-97,
132-135.

Jordan, Michael, 14-15

Knight, Bobby, 86

Maravich, Pete, 57-58

Motta, Dick, 118-122

Offcnsc
Catching, 80
Drill, Turning Against Pressure, 88-90
Driving, 99-100
Protecting The Ball, 90
Facing The Basket, 86-87
Getting The Ball, 76-77, 79
Making The Easy Play, 86

Offensive Emphasis, 102
Pivoting, 87-88
Running Hard, 79
Screening, 80-83

Passing
Fundamentals, 91-92
Types, 92-95

Practice Charts, 128-131

Practice, Example, 29

Rebounding
Drills, 69-70
Philosophy, 68
Rodman, Dennis, 77-78

Shooting
Being Ready To Shoot, 91
Form, 30-31
Free Throws, 72
Lay-Ups, 35-39
Quickness Drill, 39
Off The Pass, 62-65
Two-Line Lay-Ups, 34-35

Scrimmaging, 76, 102, 125-126

Stations, 57

Talking, 80, 98

Tryouts
    Description of, 18-25
    Getting Cut, 122

Williams, Roy, 11

Wooden, John, 99